Lots of animals have tails.
Tails can be all shapes and sizes.

a zebra's tail

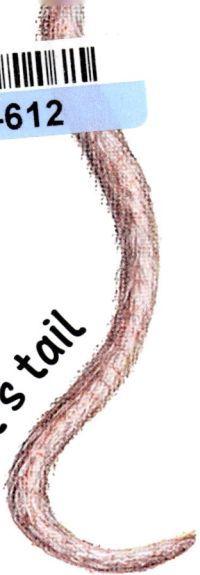

a rat's tail

a lion's tail

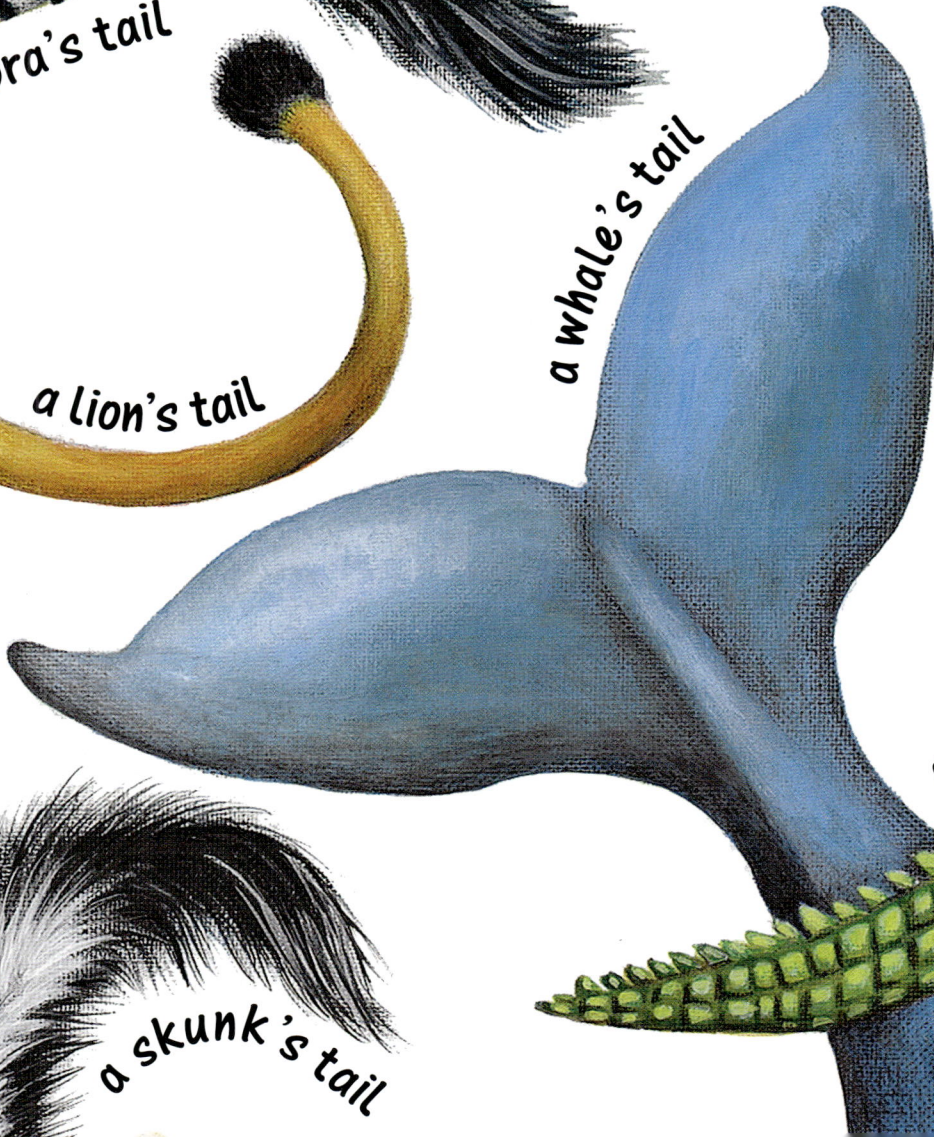

a whale's tail

a goat's tail

a crocodile's tail

a skunk's tail

1

This cat has a long black tail. She waves it when she is cross.

She fluffs it up when she sees a dog.

This kitten likes to chase its tail.

This puppy has a stumpy tail. He wags it when he is happy.

Let's play!

This rabbit has a white bobtail. It flashes when he runs.

That is a signal to run away.

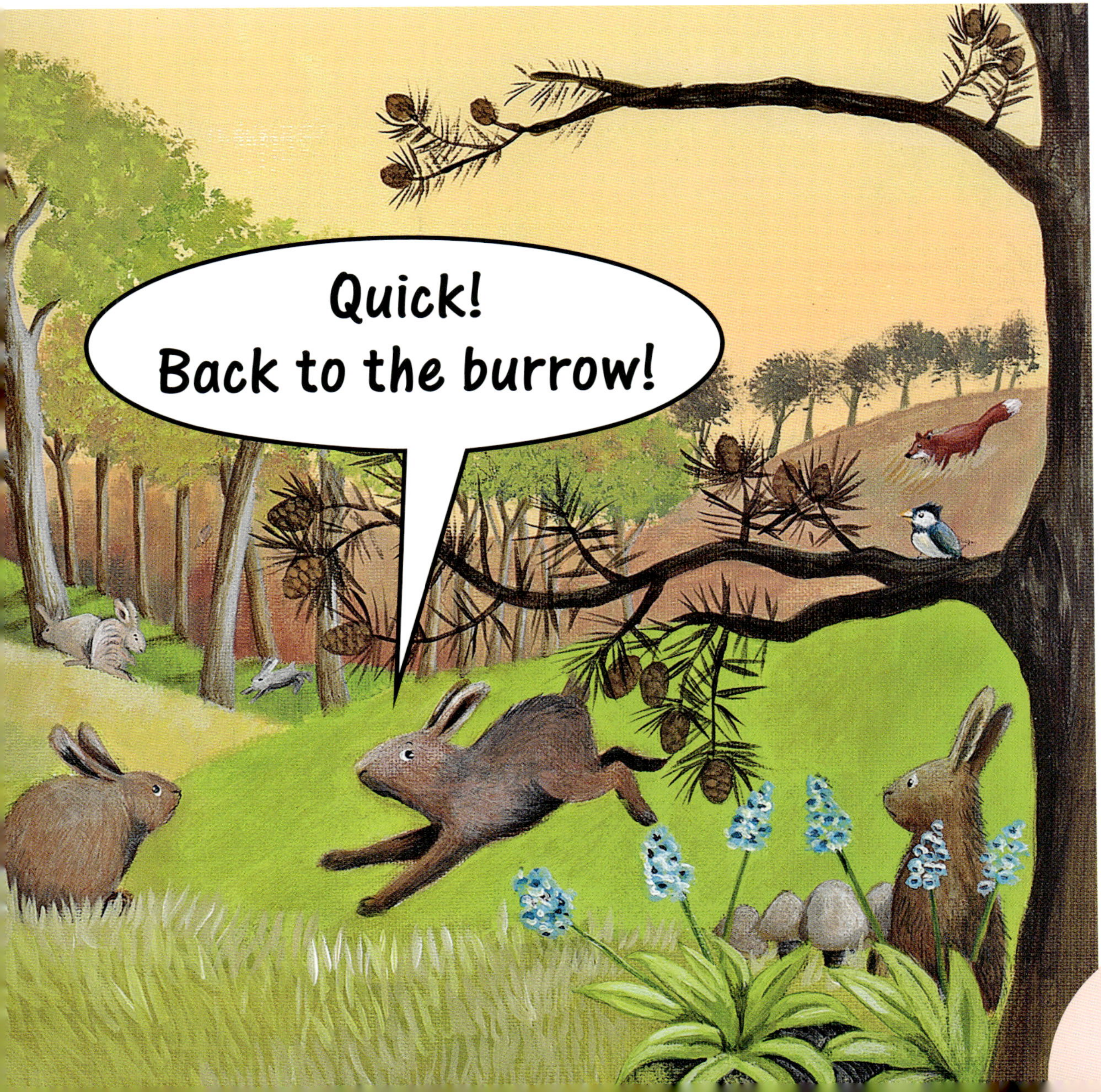
Quick!
Back to the burrow!

This squirrel has a tail like a brush.
It helps him leap.

This fox has a brush as well. So do her three cubs.

Fish have tails which help them to swim.

This stingray stings fishes with its tail. Then it eats them.

Snakes have scaly tails.

This snake kills the animals it is going to eat, by crushing them.

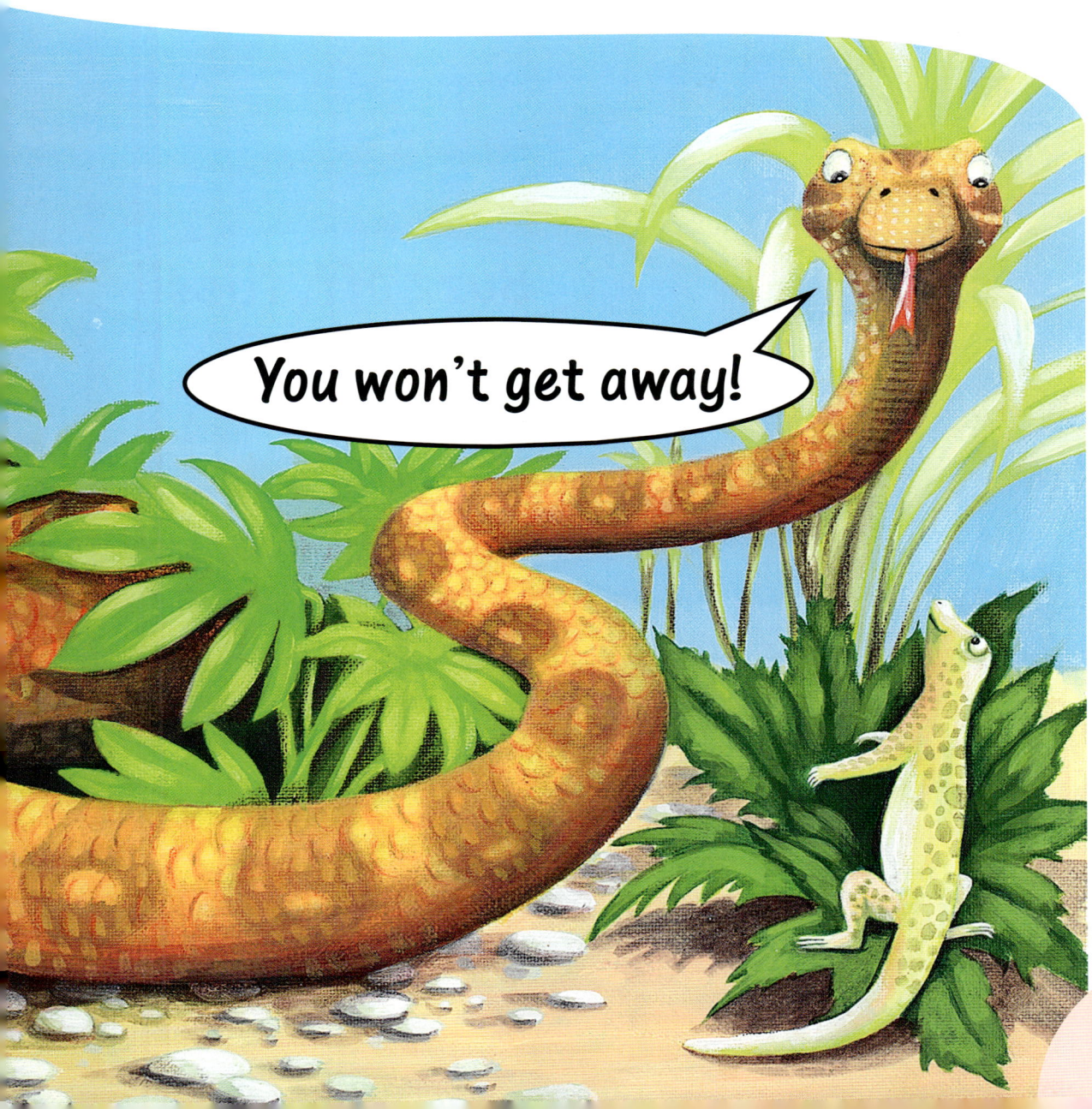

You won't get away!

This pony has a tail which can swish away flies.

This peacock has an amazing tail. He opens it up like a fan when he wants to show off.

# I wish I had a tail!